T0080594

WO

Land and Water

HEINLE CENGAGE Learning™

Y|S|G A YBM COMPANY Young & Son Global, Inc.

Do you live closer to a mountain or an ocean?

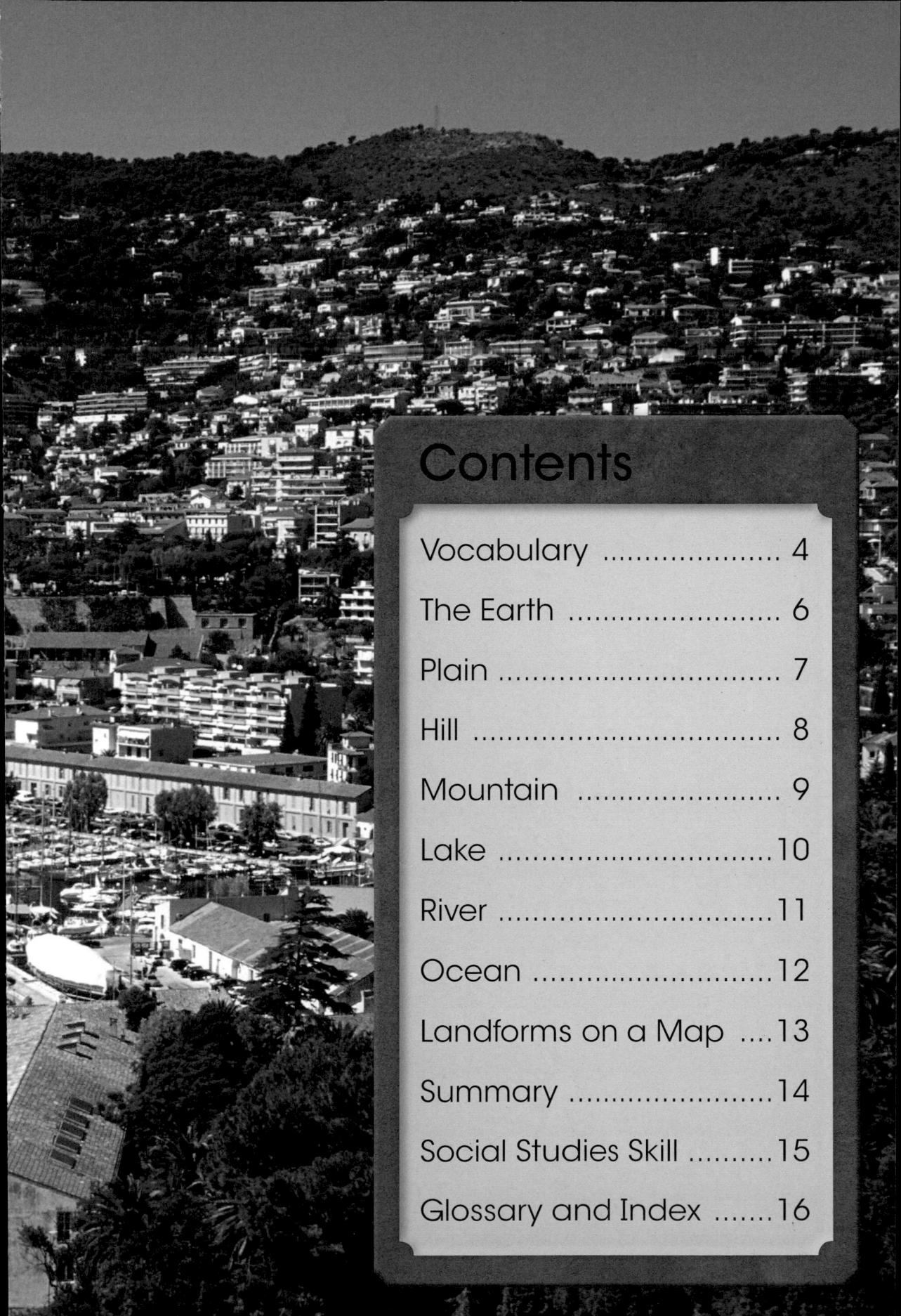

Contents

Vocabulary 4

The Earth 6

Plain 7

Hill 8

Mountain 9

Lake 10

River 11

Ocean 12

Landforms on a Map 13

Summary 14

Social Studies Skill 15

Glossary and Index 16

Vocabulary
plain
hill
mountain

lake
river
ocean

The Earth

Look at the Earth!
The blue parts are water.
The green and brown parts are land.
There are different kinds of landforms
and bodies of water on Earth.

Plain

A plain is a large, flat area of land.
Plains are often grassy.
Some plains are good for farming.

Hill

A hill is land that is higher than the land around it.
Most hills have round tops.

The Himalayas, Nepal

Mountain

Mountains are much higher than hills. They are the highest kind of land on Earth. Mountains are often steep and rocky.

Lake

A lake is a body of water that has land on all sides.

Most lakes have fresh water.

River

A river is a long body of fresh water. Rivers carry water across the land. They flow into lakes, other rivers, or oceans.

Ocean

An ocean is the largest body of water. Unlike most lakes and rivers, oceans are made of salt water.

Oceans cover most of the Earth.

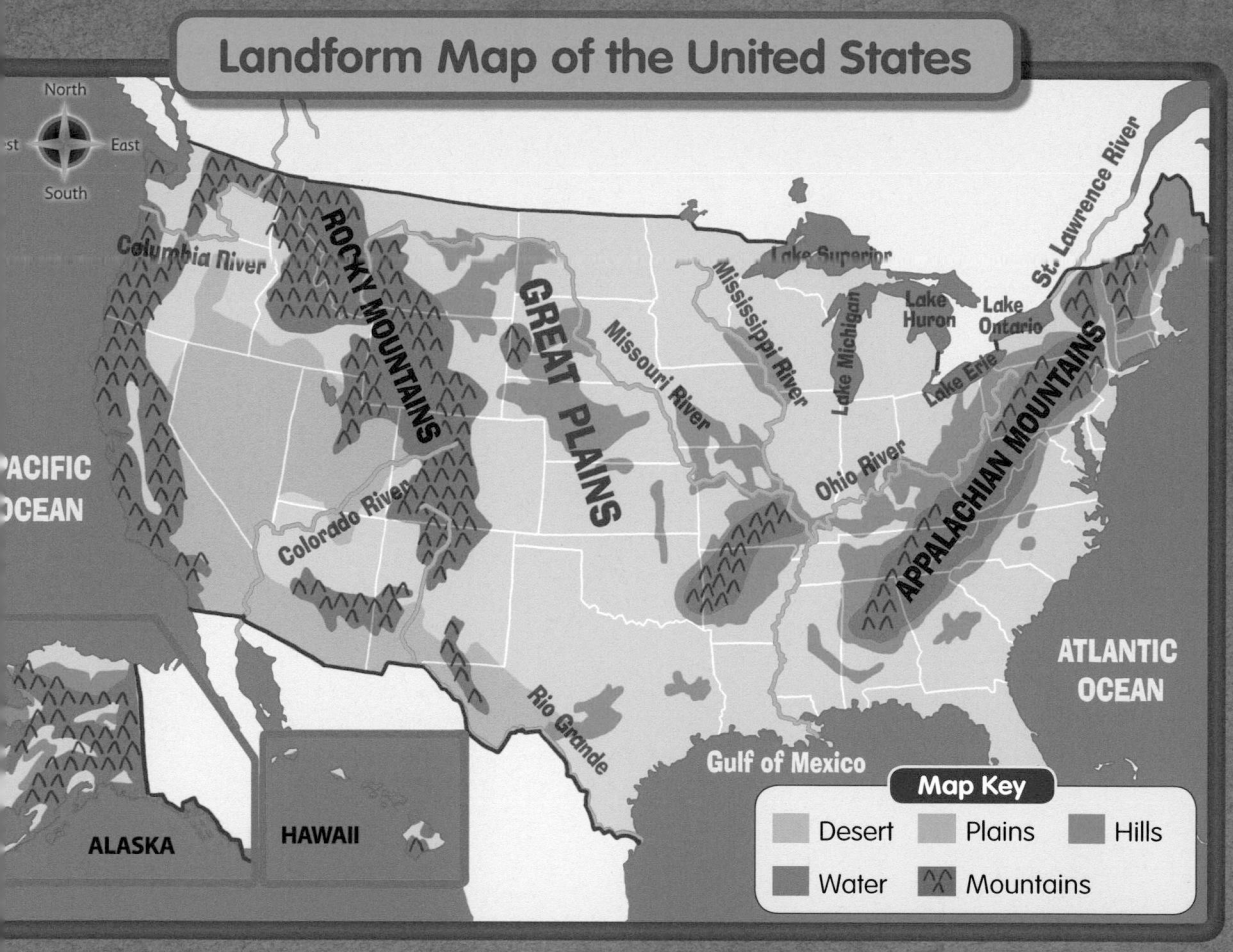

The Earth's surface is different from place to place.

Summary

What are these types of land and water?

Social Studies Skill

Read a Landform Map

A **landform map** uses colors and symbols to show different kinds of land.

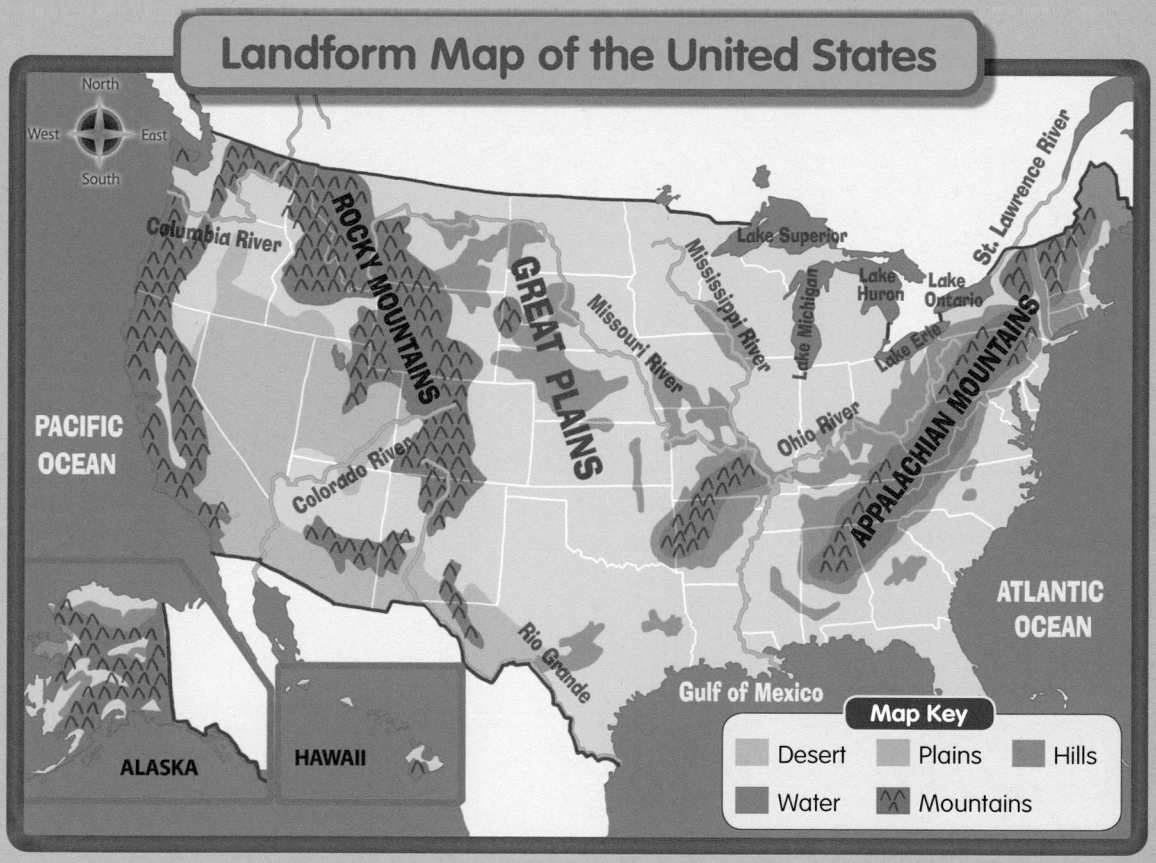

1. What does the orange part show?
2. What kinds of landforms are there in Alaska?
3. Are there more plains or mountains in the United States?

Glossary

flow
To move smoothly and continuously in one direction

fresh water
Water in lakes and rivers that does not contain any salt

rocky
Made of rock and therefore usually rough and difficult to travel along

steep
Rising or falling sharply

surface
The top layer or outside part of something

Index

Earth, 6, 9, 12–13
flow, 11
fresh water, 10–11
grassy, 7
hill, 8–9
lake, 10–12
land, 6–11
mountain, 9
oceans, 11–12
plain, 7
river, 11–12
rocky, 9
round, 8
salt water, 12
steep, 9
surface, 13
water, 6, 10–12